FANTAIL

Compiled and edited by Rod Green

RED NOSE JOKE BOOK

Illustrations by
Kim Blundell
Ainslie Macleod
Dave Crook
Rod Green
Anna Brockett

ISBN 0140 900 357

Fantail Publishing,
an imprint of Puffin Enterprises.

Published by the Penguin Group,
27 Wrights Lane,
London W8 5TZ,
England.

First published 1989.
13 5 7 9 10 8 6 4 2

Type set by
Fullpoint Filmsetting Limited.

Made and printed in Great Britain by
William Clowes Limited
Beccles and London

FOREWAD

"Dunplastering"
Wealthy Geezers Lane
London Borough of Extremely Richmond

Dear You Lot,
It's me — £oadsamoney an' I've been asked to do the introduction to this book 'cos I'm totally great, of course. You lot are great 'n all, 'cos you've bought this book, but not as great as me 'cos I'm the greatest bloke in the world — so there!

Anyway, there's £oadsajokes in this book and they're all almost as great as me, but not quite. There's £oadsadifferentsections. There's nonsense jokes like "Hello, my name's £oadsamoney and I'm stoney broke." That's nonsense, innit — I've got **£OADSAMONEY!**

There's Knock!Knock! jokes too. Here's one I've written.
You — Knock!Knock!
LOADSAMONEY — What d'you want?
You — No, you're supposed to say "Who's there?"
LOADSAMONEY — Shut your mouth and go away — I don't care what your name is 'cos I've got £oadsamoney!

Good, eh? There's also policeman jokes. I got stopped by the Bill the other day for speedin' in my motor — got fined 200 quid — so I took me wad out and gave him it straight away. Oh, yeah! I always pay the Bill in cash! Ha! Ha! Ha!

There's school jokes too. Here's one from my school days.

MATHS TEACHER — Loadsapocketmoney! What's $1 + 4 + 8 + 7 + 210 + 2 + 728 + 110$?

ME — Sir! $1 + 4 + 8 + 7 + 210 + 2 + 728 + 110 =$ LOADS!! And sir?

MATHS TEACHER — Yes, Loadsapocketmoney?

ME — How come you've got such a big nose?

MATHS TEACHER — Go and see the Headmaster!

ME — Shut your mouth! Ha! Ha! Ha!

I like animal jokes — i.e. What's round and prickly and red all over?

Answer — A hedgehog after I've squashed it in me motor! Yuk! Yuk! Yuk!

There's £oadsaletters in this book apart from mine which is, of course, the best. They're all from geezers complaining about the brilliant jokes. We should have said "Shut your mouths!" and stuffed their letters in the bin, but we printed them instead for you lot to laugh at!

Well, I don't want to write any more now — I've got some plastering to do — so you lot can shut your mouths and read this book!

£oadsamoney

£oadsamoney

53¾ Smorgasbord Avenue,
Sniggeringham,
Fallingover,
Herts.

Dear Sir or Madman,

When I first heard with my very own eyes that you were including a load of utter uousəusə in this book I could not believe what I was seeing on the telephone. What I was seeing on the telephone was, in fact, a bluebottle with a red nose.

The bluebottle had flown straight into my recently completed painting of a red five pound note. Had it been a redbottle flying into a painting of a blue five pound note my forgery would not have been so easily spotted and the police would not at this very moment be breaking down my front door.

In any case, when I learned of your disgraceful uousəusə jokes I completely lost my temper. Eventually I found it upstairs slamming doors and ripping off the wallpaper in the hall.

As a fully qualified Professor of Paranonsensical Science with a degree in Advanced Armadillo Droppings, I feel that proper uousəusə is not to be taken lightly. Indeed, it should be taken three times a day after meals, but that's not much use to me as the local constabulary have just entered the room and I have nothing with which to defend myself except a razor sharp crust of toast left over from breakfast.

Briefly, and this will have to be brief as it's not too easy to write whilst wearing handcuffs and being dragged into a police van, I find your uousəusə jokes entirely on pages 5-15 and wish to register disgust with all your other jokes too, apart from the one about the three-headed policeman which I rather liked. Actually, I have reason to believe that he's just arrested me.

Yours arrestedly,

Prof. Angus Millicent Herringbone-Treestump III

NONSENSICAL NOTIONS!

How do you get rid of flies in the kitchen?
Dump a ton of dung in the living room!

What lives in the ground and holds up stage coaches?
Dick Turnip!

What do you get if you cross a skunk with a TV?
Smellyvision.

What do you get if you cross a lock with a puppet?
Pinokeyhole!

What goes **ZZUB-ZZUB-ZZUB?**
A bee flying backwards.

What moves across the grass going
PUTT-PUTT-PUTT-PUTT-PUTT?
A bad golfer.

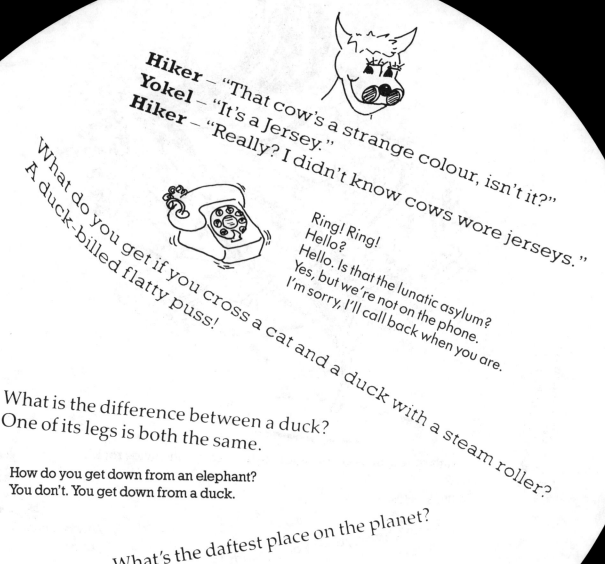

Hiker – "That cow's a strange colour, isn't it?"
Yokel – "It's a Jersey."
Hiker – "Really? I didn't know cows wore jerseys."

Ring! Ring!
Hello?
Hello. Is that the lunatic asylum?
Yes, but we're not on the phone.
I'm sorry, I'll call back when you are.

What do you get if you cross a cat and a duck with a steam roller?
A duck-billed flatty puss!

What is the difference between a duck?
One of its legs is both the same.

How do you get down from an elephant?
You don't. You get down from a duck.

What's the daftest place on the planet?

Twitzerland

What pudding moans a lot?
A rhubarb grumble!

What's green, lives at the bottom of the garden and sings rock 'n' roll?
Elvis Parsley.

What's brown, pongs and sounds like a bell?
Dung.

Why is a crow?
Caws.

Why can't you give a dying rabbit the kiss of life?

He can only be saved by a hare's breath.

What does a hockey team do when it rains?
It gets wet.

What's black and lies around a garage forecourt reciting
Shakespeare?
Refined oil!

HIKER – "What's the quickest way to the railway station?"
YOKEL – "Run."

What do you get if you cross a puddle with a pair of sandals?
Wet feet!

What's black and shoots out of the desert screaming
"Knickers! Knickers! Knickers!"
Crude oil.

A brand new Rolls Royce pulled up outside a little pub and the
proud owner strolled into the bar to tell his mates all about his
flashy new motor.
"It's got leather seats, air conditioning, electric windows,
electric sunroof, electric everything-else-you-can-think-of and

WATCH DOG

Husband – "Wow! That was some fishing trip! I've brought back two haddock, three plaice, one trout and a panfor!"

Wife – "What's a panfor?"

Husband – "It's for you to cook the fish in!"

How do you make alphabet soup thicker?
Add more Ps.

Horse Fly

My horse can jump a six foot fence.
That's nothing! My pony can jump higher than my house. Mind you, my house can't jump very high...

---

a television and drinks cabinet in the back. In fact, the back seat is so big that I can lie down on it and have a nap if I'm tired," he boasted.

"So what?" said a little bloke in the corner. "I've got all that stuff in my old mini AND the rear seat folds down into a double bed

What's pink but near to silver?
The Lone Ranger's bum!

Husband: What's for tea?
Wife: We're having fish fingers for a change.
Husband: So these are fish fingers? Wow! That must have been some fish!

so that I can sleep there all night if I want to."
Flabbergasted by the little man's claims, the Rolls Royce owner immediately returned his Roller to the factory and had it converted at a cost of several thousand pounds to have the rear seat fold down into a king size bed with a dressing table and wardrobe built in.

What do you call a man with jelly in one ear and custard and fruit in the other?
A trifle deaf!

Once all the work was completed he returned to the pub and spotted the little man's mini parked outside. The windows were steamed up, so he knocked on the roof. The little man's face appeared at the window.

"What do you want?" he said.

A man walks in to a theatrical agent's office one day and tells the secretary that he has a marvellous new act for the agent to see. The secretary shows him into the boss's office.

"Well, what's this marvellous new act you're going to show me?" says the agent.

"It's this," says the man, producing a frog from his pocket and placing it on the agent's desk. From another pocket, he brings out a small piano which he sets down in front of the frog. Immediately, the frog starts to play the piano. Amazed by the incredible frog, the agent realises that the act could be worth millions, but decides to bargain with the man to buy the frog cheaply.

"Hmm," says the agent. "The frog's quite good, really, but he needs something else to liven up his act."

"No problem," says the man and takes a mouse from another pocket. The mouse scampers across the desk, climbs up onto the piano and starts to sing "Move Over Darling." The agent is astounded and the secretary can't believe her eyes.

"Okay," he says craftily, "I'll give you two hundred pounds for the act."

"Done!" says the man. The agent gives him the cash and secretary shows him out.

"You're mad," she says. "That act must have been worth much more than two hundred pounds."

"No, it's all a trick," whispers the man. "The mouse can't sing at all – the frog's a ventriloquist!"

OLD LADY – "Have you put the cat out yet, dear?"
OLD MAN – "I didn't even know he was on fire!"

What's black and dangles from the light socket?
A careless electrician.

"I just thought I'd let you know that my back seat now folds down into a king size bed with a built-in wardrobe and dressing table!" bragged the Roller owner.

"What?" gasped the little man. "You mean you got me out of the jacuzzi just to tell me that?"

A LOONY

Walking past the house of a local nut case, a woman spots the loony sitting on his front lawn leaning forward and pulling back as though rowing a boat.
"What on earth are you doing?" she asks.
"I'm rowing this boat across the lake."
"But there's no boat there."
"Help! Help! I can't swim!"

Who said;
"Get stuffed hairy face! Call yourself a wolf, dog breath? My pet gerbil's more ferocious than you, you wally!"

Little Rude Riding Hood.

What has fifty legs but can't walk?
25 pairs of trousers.

A soldier on his first parachute jump leapt from a plane 10,000 ft up and plummeted towards the earth. He got a bit of a shock when his parachute failed to open but he knew he had a reserve parachute. To open the reserve he had to pull on a cord, but when he pulled it, the cord snapped off in his hand.
"Oh, no!" he screamed. "What do I do now?"
Then, as he plunged through the air he passed a man going upwards carrying a spanner and smoking a cigarette.
"Know anything about parachutes?" yelled the soldier.
"'Fraid not, mate," said the man. "Know anything about gas cookers?"

Little Girl — "Where are you taking all that dung?"
Gardener — "I'm going to put it on my rhubarb."
Little Girl — "Yeeuch!! We have custard on ours!"

HMM - MMM - M

Why do bees hum?
Because they can't remember the words.

Bore – "Did I tell you that I only weighed 2½ lbs when I was born?"
Bored – "Really? Did you live?"
Bore – "Not half! You should see me now!"

MOTHER: See that tall lady, Sarah? She's six feet in her socks!
SARAH: Come off it, Mum! You'll be telling me next she's three heads in her hat!

Two workmen were installing a plate glass window in a shop. Before they could fit the new glass, they had to remove all the old broken glass. As they were doing this a large chunk of glass fell from the top of the window frame and chopped off one of the workmen's ears.

"Aaaaargh!" screamed the unfortunate workman.

"What's wrong?" asked his mate.

"That falling glass just chopped me ear off!" howled the injured man.

"Is this it?" asked his mate picking up a severed ear.

"I don't think so," groaned the wounded workman. "Mine had a pencil behind it."

Hiker – "How far is it to the nearest town?"
Yokel – "'Bout five miles as the crow flies."
Hiker – "How far if the crow has to walk and carry an enormous rucksack?"

WAITER! WAITER!

Fwilty Towers Hotle,
Torkee,
Defon.

Dear Signor Red Nose,
    Whatta you mean by take ze Mickee from hard whorking whayters? Ees not ver nice when you make weeth ze Whayter! Whayter! fun-type laughs all ze times!
    Seence I ees coming here from Barcelona I ees whorking as whayter hand ees not many laughs I ees having, let me tell you! I ees whorking twentee seex hours in day for not so much monee, hand a smack on ze head!
    You say, "Ha-ho! Ees funnee yoking!"
    But I say, "Que?"
    Only laughs I ees having weeth your Nosey Red Book of Yokings ees weeth ze yokings habout ze teachers. Ees reminding me of ze persons who have teach me English so good.

    Yours seencerely,

Manuel

Waiter! Waiter! This waffle's awful!
You've just eaten a place mat, sir.

Waiter! Waiter! This pudding's awful!
What's wrong with it?
Well, the custard's almost thick enough to get a job here!

Waiter! Waiter! I'd like a beef stroganoff!
Sorry, sir, we don't have enough strogs!

Waiter! Waiter! This ice cream is all squashed!
Yes, sir. You told me to bring your dessert and step on it!

Waiter! Waiter! Where's my honey?
She left last Thursday, sir!

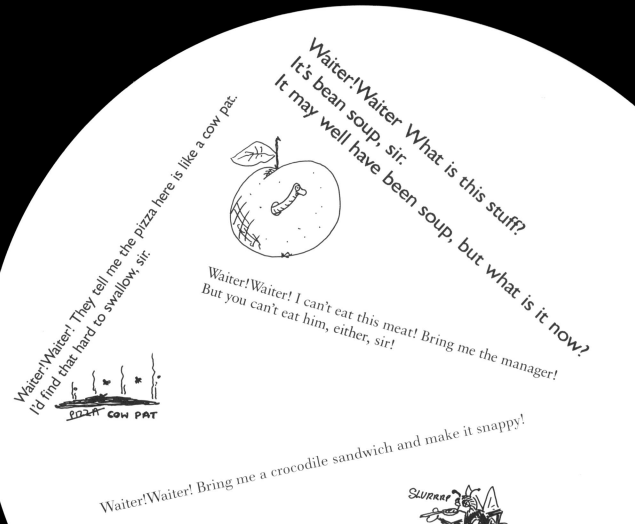

Waiter! Waiter! What is this stuff?
It's bean soup, sir.
It may well have been soup, but what is it now?

Waiter! Waiter! They tell me the pizza here is like a cow pat.
I'd find that hard to swallow, sir.

PIZZA COW PAT

Waiter! Waiter! I can't eat this meat! Bring me the manager!
But you can't eat him, either, sir!

Waiter! Waiter! Bring me a crocodile sandwich and make it snappy!

SLURRRP

Waiter! Waiter! There's a fly in my soup!
Well, he won't drink much, will he sir?

Waiter! Waiter! There's a fly in my soup!
Never mind, sir, the spider on the bread will get 'im!

Waiter! Waiter! How long will my sausages be?
About four inches, sir!

Waiter! Waiter! What are these two flies doing in my soup?
Synchronised swimming, sir. Don't they have lovely smiles?

Waiter! Waiter! You've got your thumb on my steak!
Don't want me to drop it again, do you?

Waiter! Waiter! There's soup in my flies!

Waiter! Waiter! This fish smells like a sweaty foot!
Well, it is a Dover sole, sir!

Waiter! Waiter! This plate is wet!
That's your soup, sir!

Waiter! Waiter! Do you recommend the fish soup?
Only when it's goin' off an' we want rid of it!

**Waiter! Waiter! Do you serve crabs?
Of course, sir, we serve anyone!**

Waiter! Waiter! Do you know how long I've been sitting here?
No, sir, but if you sing it, I'll join in the chorus!

Waiter! Waiter! What's this beetle doing marching through my mince?
About 2 mph, sir!

Waiter! Waiter! I'd like a greasy plate of burned chips, frozen solid peas and a
hamburger with a thumbprint on it and a fingernail on top.
We don't serve food like that, sir!
You did yesterday!

Waiter! Waiter! I'd like a stewed telegraph pole with truck tyres and roof tiles, please.
Boss! the loony's back again!

YES, IT'S
HIM AGAIN! →

Waiter! Waiter! Why's that chap howling like a dog?
He's the whine waiter, sir!

Waiter! Waiter! Why's there a piece of rubber in my shepherd's pie?
Maybe it's part of the shepherd's wellies, sir!

Waiter! Waiter! Do you have frog's legs?
No, sir, but I've got pig's trotters!

Waiter! Waiter! I'd like a steak and a cup of tea.
Fillet?
Yes, right up to the brim!

Waiter! Waiter! there's a fly paddling in my soup!
Don't you mean swimming, sir?
No, you didn't give me enough soup for that!

Waiter! Waiter! Do you have frog's legs?
Yes, sir.
Well hop over to the kitchen and get me a steak!

Waiter! Waiter! Why are you poking around in my stew?
Well, you don't want to swallow my glass eye, do you?

Waiter! Waiter! There's a worm on my plate!
That's your sausage, sir!

Waiter! Waiter! Do you have chicken legs?
No, sir, it's just the way I walk!

Waiter! Waiter! That cat just licked all the gravy off my plate in 3 seconds flat!
Gosh, sir! That's a new lap record!

Waiter! Waiter! I loved the beef surprise, but what's the surprise?
It was dog food, sir!

Waiter! Waiter! I'm in a big hurry, but I'll have the duck.
Certainly, sir, and shall I do.
No, just a leg or a wing will bring the bill?

Waiter! Waiter! Is this chicken fresh?
Fresh? It just pecked me!

Waiter! Waiter! I'd like you to call me a taxi.
Okay – YOU'RE A TAXI!!

Waiter! Waiter! Can I smoke here?
You can burst into flames for all I care!

Waiter! There's no chicken in the chicken pie!
Well, sir, there's no shepherd in the shepherd's pie or cottage
in the cottage pie, either!

Waiter!Waiter! This meat is raw!
No it's not, sir!
Yes, it is! I've seen cows hurt worse than this and live!

Waiter!Waiter! This egg is rotten!
Don't blame me, sir, I only laid the table!

HEY, YOU! SEEN A GIRL CALLED MUFFET?

Waiter!Waiter! Why is there a spider drowning in my soup?
Because they're not very good swimmers, sir!

Waiter!Waiter! I'd like apple tart without cream.
Sorry, sir, we don't have any cream – but you can have it without custard!

Waiter!Waiter! Why's that chap carrying a tray of skulls?
He's the head waiter, sir!

999 Letsbee Avenue,
Cuffson,
Runimin,
PC9 99Z.

Dear Sir/Madam,

Acting on information received, I examined pages 28 and 29 of the Comic Relief Red Nose Joke Book and discovered several "jokes" and a "humorous drawing" acting in a suspicious manner.

I proceeded in an orderly and carefully numbered direction to pages 32 and 33 where my suspicions were confirmed — the Law and Disorder chapter contains "jokes" and "humorous drawings" loitering with intent to make people laugh and conspiring to cause grievous embarrassment to officers of the law.

Having secured evidence of these offences, it is now my considered opinion that the guilty parties be dealt with severely. The following are my recommendations for sentencing:

Jokes about Constables — A stiff lecture and a small fine.

Jokes about Sergeants — A large fine and/or imprisonment.

Jokes about Inspectors — Immediate imprisonment and/or hanging.

Jokes about Chief Supers — No sentence, everyone makes jokes about Chief Supers.

Jokes about Chief Constables — Hanging, electric chair and/or firing squad.

It is totally unacceptable that members of the public should be exposed to page after page containing jokes about police officers, although some of the jokes about stupid doctors are pretty good.

Yours policingly,

Ivor Truncheon (6437)
Chief Constable Ivor Truncheon

Policeman – "Hey, you! Didn't I just see you finding a five pound note?"
Little girl – "Yes, sir."
Policeman – "But you're not going to keep it, are you?"
Little girl – "No, sir."
Policeman – "And what are you going to do with it?"
Little girl – "Spend it!"

A policeman staggered into the station wearing nothing but his shirt and boxer shorts.

"What on earth happened to you?" asked the sergeant.

"I've been mugged, Sarge," gasped the policeman. "They took my uniform, my helmet, my radio, my boots, all my money and my watch!"

"Weren't you carrying your truncheon?" the sergeant asked.

"Yes, Sarge!" said the policeman, producing the truncheon from inside his shirt. "But I managed to hide that from them!"

Recruit – "What will I be when I pass all me exams, Sarge?"
Sergeant – "A pensioner, probably!"

What does the laughing motorcycle policeman ride?
A Yamaha-ha or a Suzuki-hee-hee!

POLICE SLIPPERS ↓

A policeman caught a little boy stealing sweets from a shop and as the shamefaced youngster stood in front of him, the policeman produced his notebook.

"Name?" he asked.

"Zacharia Osnastrinski Kristianolowski, sir," said the little boy.

"Well," said the policeman, putting away his notebook. "Don't let me catch you at it again!"

TRAMP BOX

Sergeant: Drunk and disorderly, eh? Okay where do you live?

Tramp: I sleep in a pig pen.

Sergeant: Cor! What about the smell?

Tramp: Oh, the pigs don't mind!

I've got a job for the flying squad!
You do?
Yes – I've lost my budgie!

What's blue and woolly and goes "Ha-ha-ha-ha-ha-ha-ha-ha-ha-ha!"
The laughing fleeceman!

What's blue, has two legs and flies?
A policeman's trousers!

How do you call the police in Australia?
Dial 666!

What do policemen have in their sandwiches?
Truncheon meat!

**Why do traffic wardens have yellow bands round their hats?
To stop people parking on their heads!**

What did the three headed policeman say?
'Ello, 'ello, 'ello! What's goin' on 'ere, then, 'ere then, 'ere then?

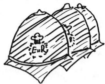

Two judges were arrested for speeding and when they came to court they were the only judges around so they had to try each other.

"You are charged with speeding," said the first judge to the one in the dock. "How do you plead?"

"Guilty," came the reply.

"I fine you £50," said the first judge.

The two men then changed places.

"You are charged with speeding," said the second judge. "How do you plead?"

"Guilty," came the reply.

"Well," said the second judge, "I find this absolutely intolerable. This is the second case like this we've had in court today and it's becoming far too common. I therefore fine you £500 and ten days in jail!"

**What happens if you try to leave a restaurant without paying?
They send for The Bill!**

Tea time at the policeman's house:-
Mum – "Okay, who wants chips?"
Kids – "Me-ma! Me-ma! Me-ma! Me-ma!"

What did the police do when burglars stole all the toilets from New Scotland Yard?
Nothing – they didn't have a thing to go on!

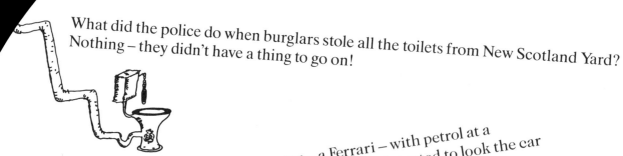

A car thief was filling his latest stolen motor – a Ferrari – with petrol at a filling station when a policeman came wandering in and started to look the car over. He took off his jacket and bent over to have a look underneath. The car thief panicked, leapt into the Ferrari and roared off. He was doing fifty miles an hour when the policeman raced past him on foot, sprinting for all he was worth. The thief put his foot down and overtook the policeman at eighty miles an hour only to have the policeman burst past him again, running like a train. Accelerating to one hundred miles an hour, the thief was astounded to see the policeman come screaming past him again, his legs a blur. The flabbergasted car thief could stand no more and slowed to a halt at the side of the road. Breathless, the policeman leant against the car door. "Thank goodness you've stopped, sir," he gasped. "I had me braces caught in your bumper!"

What did the police do when there was a mass escape from Battersea Dogs' Home?
Nothing – they didn't have any leads!

The world's worst forger was arrested by police when he tried to buy a new car with 1,000 nine pound notes.

Sheriff: Be on the look out for three cowboys wearing paper undies.
Deputy: What are they wanted for?
Sheriff: Rustlin'!

What did the policeman say when he walked into a bar?
"**OUCH!**" It was a iron bar.

Sergeant – "What did the suspect look like?"
Recruit – "He had a thick brown beard."
Sergeant – "A Naval beard?"
Recruit – "No, it was just on his face!"

Ring! Ring!
Hello, is that the police station?
Yes, madam.
What are you doing about the hole that's been drilled in the wall of the nudist camp?
We're looking in to it, madam!

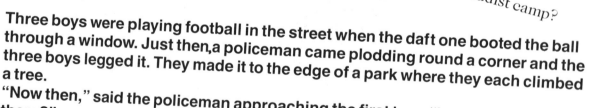

Three boys were playing football in the street when the daft one booted the ball through a window. Just then, a policeman came plodding round a corner and the three boys legged it. They made it to the edge of a park where they each climbed a tree.

"Now then," said the policeman approaching the first tree. "Is there anyone up there?"

Thinking fast, the first boy said "Cheep-Cheep!" like a little bird. Satisfied that there was only a bird up that tree, the policeman moved on to the next tree.

"Now then," he said. "Is there anyone up there?"

"Miaow!" said the second boy, just like a cat.

Standing under the tree where the wally hid, the policeman said:

"Now then. Is there anyone up there?"

"Mooooooo . . ."

Sergeant – "Is this your truncheon? The name's obliterated."
Recruit – "Can't be mine, Sarge. My name's Plod."

Policeman: I'm looking for a man with one leg called Long John Silver.
Pirate: Really? What's his other leg called?

Judge (at dentist's) – "Do you promise to remove the tooth, the whole tooth and nothing but the tooth?"

What do you call a blackbird who joins the police force?
A rookie!

Policeman – "Hey, boy! What are you doing with that line of penguins following you? I told you to take them to the zoo yesterday!"

Boy – "I did, and they loved it! Today I'm taking them to the pictures!"

What did the policeman's left boot say to his right boot after he'd taken them off? "We haven't got a copper between us!"

What has four legs and goes "**Munch-mutter-munch-mutter-munch-mutter**

A motorcycle cop was cruising along a quiet country road when an old lady sped past him in a beaten up old car. To his astonishment, she was knitting as she hurtled along. He raced alongside her, drawing level with her open window at 110mph.

"Pull over!" he yelled.

"No," smiled the old lady, "it's a cardigan, actually!"

What's the difference between a Chief Inspector and a pennin?

What's a pennin?

Not much. What's 'appenin wiv you?

In the courtroom the judge was amazed to see a vicar in the dock before him.

"What on earth have you been up to, Vicar?" he asked.

"I was riding my bicycle up the wrong lane of a dual carriageway, Your Honour."

"That's very serious. I'll have to fine you $50," said the judge. "Weren't you frightened you would be killed?"

"No," said the vicar. "The Lord was with me."

"In that case," said the judge. "I fine you another $50 for having two on a bike!"

Policeman – "What's in that sack?"

Villain – "Er … rhubarb!"

Policeman – "In that case, I'll have to take you into custardy!"

munch-mutter?" **Two policemen eating sandwiches in a bus shelter!**

Sergeant – "What would you do if you were in a patrol car being chased by armed thugs doing 80mph?"

Recruit – "90mph!"

Sergeant – "And what steps would you take if there was a man-eating tiger on the loose?"

Recruit – "Large, fast ones!"

AN APPLE A DAY...

Dear Sir,

Harley Street,
London.

I am a Doctor. Open wide. Say "AAH." Now say "PLOP." Now say "KANGAROO-TURBAN-BLUBBER-WOMBAT."

How are you feeling now? You should be feeling like a complete wally, which is precisely how I felt when I saw the incredibly insulting Doctor jokes in the "Apple A Day" section of your Red Nose Joke Book!!

Believe me, a red nose (brought about by a swift punch up the hooter) is exactly what you'd have if I could get my hands on you at this very moment! I'll be letting all my Doctor friends know about your disgraceful book, so next time you go to see your Doctor, you'd better watch out! You could start off with a slight cold and end up with bubonic plague and an amputated head!! You have been warned!

Yours furiously,

Dr. A. Pendix

Dr A. Pendix

P.S. Loved the Waiter! Waiter! jokes.

Doctor! Doctor! I keep thinking I'm an elephant!
Take these tablets.
What are they?
Trunkquillizers!

Doctor! Doctor! I keep thinking I'm a pair of curtains!
Pull yourself together, man!

Doctor! Doctor! Why don't people like me?
You're stupid.
I want a second opinion!
Okay – you're ugly as well!

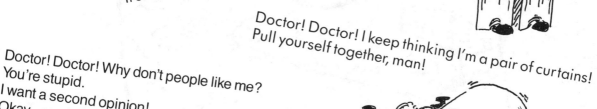

"How are we today?" smiled the doctor, visiting a patient at home.
"Not so good, doctor," moaned the bloated little man in the bed. The doctor then
spotted a full bottle of medicine lying on the bedside table.
"I told you to drink half a cupful of that every day after a hot bath," said the
doctor, "but you haven't done it, have you?"
"No, doctor," gasped the man. "There just wasn't any room for the medicine after I'd drunk the bath!"

Doctor! Doctor! Everyone keeps ignoring me!
Next please!

Doctor! Doctor! My wife thinks she's a bird!
Dear me. I'll see her straight away.
You can't. She's flown south for the winter!

A grim-faced doctor approached the hospital bed of a patient who was just waking up after an operation.

"I'm afraid we've got some bad news and some good news for you," he said. "Which would you like first?"

"T-tell me the bad news, doc," groaned the patient.

"The bad news is that we had to amputate both of your legs," said the doctor, "but the good news is that the man in the next bed wants to buy your slippers!"

Doctor! Doctor! I'm seeing double all the time!
Lie on the couch, please.
Which one?

Doctor! Doctor! I feel like a formula one racing car!
Take two of these pills every four laps!

Doctor! Doctor! I feel like a Cocktail Shaker!
What's got into you?
Gin, Martini, a little lemonade …

"Doctor, I've got a terrible problem," moaned a woman as she rushed into the doctor's surgery. "I've got horribly bad breath!"
"Come, come," said the doctor soothingly. "It can't be that bad. Lean over the desk and breathe out."
The woman gave him a blast of her sewer-like breath and the doctor collapsed under his desk with his eyebrows melting.
"You weren't joking, were you?" said the doctor, reappearing with a gas mask on.
"I recommend that you chew a tablespoonful of fresh dung every two hours."
"Will that cure my bad breath?" asked the woman.
"No," said the doctor, "but at least it will tone it down a bit!"

Doctor! Doctor! There's a fly in my soup!
Eh?

PONG!!

Doctor! Doctor! I keep losing my . . .
Keep losing your what?
Loosing my, er . . .
Losing your voice?
No, losing my, um . . .
Losing your balance?
No, losing my, mmm . . .
Losing your memory?
Yes! That's it! I keep forgetting things!
How long has this been happening?
How long has what been happening?

Doctor! Doctor! I feel like a hamburger!
So do I. Let's go down to the Wimpy!

A worried man went to see his doctor one day.
"I don't know if you can help me, doctor," he said, "but I keep getting this urge to steal things. I've been doing burglaries, shoplifting – it's awful!"
"Hmmm . . ." said the doctor, scribbling out a prescription. "Take these tablets."
"What if they don't work?" asked the man.
"Then," said the doctor, "could you try to get me a video?"

A man with sore knees went to the doctor for advice. The doctor told him that he needed to take more exercise and that he should walk at least ten miles a day for the next fortnight. Two weeks later the man's knees were fine, but he was 140 miles away!

DOCTOR'S SURGERY 140 MILES

RECEPTIONIST – Doctor, the invisible man's in the waiting room.
DOCTOR – Tell him I can't see him!

Doctor! Doctor! My husband's out in the street. He thinks he's
a Mini Metro!
I say! You'd better bring him in to see me.
I can't! He's been wheelclamped!

"Hmmm," said the world famous Harley Street doctor as he examined his patient.
"Have you had this before?"
"Yes," replied the patient.
"Well," sighed the confused doctor, "you've got it again!"

Doctor! Doctor! I feel like a racehorse!
How long has this been going on?
Ever since I won the Grand National!

DOCTOR – Are you still having trouble getting to sleep?
PATIENT – Yes, doctor.
DOCTOR – Did you try counting sheep like I said?
PATIENT – Yes, doctor. Last night I counted 692,427 sheep and three lambs.
DOCTOR – Then you fell asleep?
PATIENT – No, then it was time to get up!

Ring! Ring!
Hello.
Hello. Is that the hospital?
Yes.
Has Mrs Powell had her baby yet?
No, not yet.
It's taking so long!
Is this her first child?
No, this is her husband!

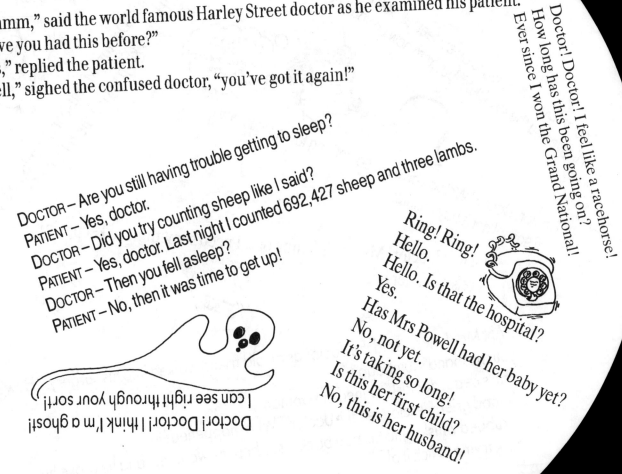

Doctor! Doctor! I think I'm a ghost!
I can see right through your sort!

Doctor! Doctor! I used to be six feet tall and now I'm only four foot six!
I'll give you these tablets, but from now on you'll have to be a little patient!

HMM.... THIS JOKE SOUNDS PRETTY WEAK TO ME!

Doctor! Doctor! Will you give me something for my little boy?
I'm sorry, I don't buy children.

DOCTOR! I THINK THIS JOKE HAS DIED!

Doctor! Doctor! My husband thinks he's Moses!
Tell him to keep taking the tablets!

Doctor! Doctor! My hair's falling out. I need something to keep it in!
Here's a carrier bag!

WIZZO

"Ah, Mrs Jones," said the doctor as an old friend walked into his surgery. "How's your husband's lumbago?"
"He's dead, doctor!" sighed the woman.
"Good grief!" exclaimed the doctor. "What happened?"
"I rubbed whisky into his bad back," sobbed the woman, "and he broke his neck trying to lick it off!"

Doctor! Doctor! What can you give me for wind?
How about a kite?

DOCTOR – My goodness! How did you come by all these scrapes and scratches?
PATIENT – I was in the desert, doc. I dived into a pond and swam 25 yards before
I realised it was a mirage!

Doctor! Doctor! I think I'm turning into a goat!
How long has this been going on?
Ever since I was a kid!

Doctor! Doctor! I keep acting like a hen!
How long has this been going on?
About six months.
What? Why didn't you come to me sooner?
We needed the eggs!

A doctor was amazed one morning to see a woman stagger into his office bent double and walking like a crab. Her body formed a perfect arch.
"You've got to help me doctor!" she pleaded. "I'm turning into a road bridge!"
"Dear me!" said the doctor. "What on earth has come over you?"
"Four cars, two motor bikes and a lorry!"

Doctor! Doctor! I think I'm a dog!
I see. Lie on the couch, will you?
I can't. I'm not allowed on the furniture!

Doctor! Doctor! I'm nineteen stones overweight!
You need to do some skipping.
You mean with a rope?
No – skip breakfast, skip lunch, skip dinner . . .

A man walked into the doctor's surgery looking flushed and feverish.
"What's up with you?" asked the doctor.
"I'm all hot and shakey and breathless," said the man.
"You must have flu," the doctor decided.
"No," said the man. "I came by bus!"

Castle Dracula,
Fang Hill,
Transylvania.

Dear Wolf-breath,

You have the brains of a sheep, the elegance of a three-legged pig and a face like a donkey's bottom!

How dare you include vampire jokes in your despicable little "joke" book! In fact, how dare you even mention our kind alongside that pathetic Frankenstein, those stupid howling werewolves and, worst of all – SWAMP MONSTERS!

I arrived home the other night just before dawn after a hard night prowling the neighbourhood. I'd only popped out for a quick bite, but did I get one? Not on your Nelly! Not even a nibble! And what had the post bat slipped under my coffin lid? Your Red Nose Joke Book! (Like the colour, by the way.)

It was the last straw. It just about drove me batty and I have now placed the dreaded curse of the vampire bat on you. Your skin will turn black, your arms will grow wings, your mouth will sprout fangs and from now on you will have to sleep hanging upside down in your wardrobe!

Unfortunately, this curse hasn't been working too well lately, but I can assure you that 400 years ago it was the business! So beware – it could strike you down at any time up to October 14 when it will probably be past its best.

That will teach you to mess with us, you miserable insect! I spit on your vampire jokes ... but I quite liked the Knock! Knock! ones.

Yours terrifyingly,

Arthur Dracula

Arthur Dracula (Count)

What's wrapped in greaseproof paper and shoots up and down the bell ropes in a French cathedral?
The lunchpack of Notre Dame!

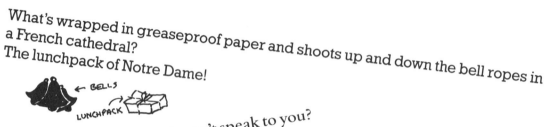

← BELLS
LUNCHPACK

What's green, eight feet tall and won't speak to you?
The Incredible Sulk!

Dracula swooped across a park at dead of night and, even though vampires have notoriously bad eyesight, he spotted one of his batty friends slumped on a park bench. As he approached, he could see that his chum was covered in blood. He landed beside his friend, thinking that he must have found a fine crop of fresh victims.

"Where have you been?" asked Dracula.

"Nowhere," replied his friend.

"Well how did you get in this state?" Dracula asked.

"See that tree over there?" moaned his friend.

"No," said Dracula.

"Neither did I!"

What's a vegetarian zombie's favourite soup?
Scream of mushroom!

← SCREAM

MUSHROOM →

AAAAAHH!!

INCREDIBLE HULK – "You look like a million dollars."
MRS HULK – "You mean I look wonderful?"
INCREDIBLE HULK – "No – you're all green and wrinkly!"

PETROL

2134

MARTIAN

MARTIAN

FLYING SAUCER

FALLING CUP

The earthling won't talk. He just stands there with his finger in his ear!

Mummy! Mummy! What's a werewolf?
Shut up and comb your face!

1ST GHOST – "My girlfriend's a medium."
2ND GHOST – "Really? Mine's a 32!"

Where do zombies go swimming?
The Dead Sea!

Frankenstein's monster and the Incredible Hulk went duck hunting with their retriever dogs. After several hours the ducks were still flying overhead and neither Frankenstein's monster nor the Hulk had got one.
"I think I know what's wrong!" said the Hulk.
"What?" asked Frankenstein's monster.
"We're not throwing the dogs high enough!"

What does Dracula get through the post?
Fang mail!

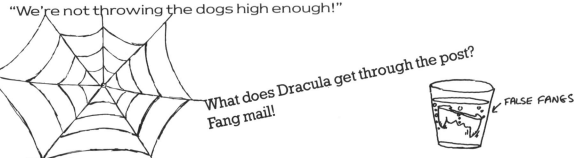

← FALSE FANGS

What do very old pixies have to do their housework?
A gnome help!

What do you get if you cross a policeman with a ghost?
An inspectre!

What position does a zombie play in a football team?
He's the ghoulie!

1ST GHOST – "I'm the best ghost you'll ever meet."
2ND GHOST – "Really?"
1ST GHOST – "Yeah. I used to specialise in frightening two-headed guardsmen
away from Edinburgh Castle."
2ND GHOST – "But you don't get two-headed guardsmen at Edinburgh Castle!"
1ST GHOST – "Told you I was good!"

A group of tourists was being shown around Notre Dame Cathedral. Quasimodo gave a demonstration of bell ringing after which all the tourists congratulated him on a fine performance, except for one.

"Pathetic!" said a little skinny bloke. "I can ring the bells in our village church better than that."

"Very well," said Quasimodo. "If you think you can do better, why don't you have a go?"

So the little man took over the bell ropes and rang the cathedral bells far better than Quasimodo had done. The hunchback was furious.

"Come with me!" he roared. "I can ring the bells in a way that you could never match!"

Together they climbed the great bell tower and when they reached the top they stood either side of the largest bell.

"Watch this!" said Quasimodo. He butted the bell with his forehead, producing the most beautiful ringing tone.

"That's nothing!" said the little skinny bloke and immediately he head butted the giant bell on his side. The tone produced was even better than the hunchback's.

Incensed, Quasimodo gripped the rim of the bell and swung it up sharply into the little bloke's face. There was a loud clang and the skinny chap was knocked off balance and clean out of the bell tower. He landed in the street hundreds of feet below. Quasimodo rushed down to the street and by the time he got there a crowd had gathered.

"What a terrible accident," said one of the bystanders. "Does anyone know who the poor man was?"

"Can't think of his name," said Quasimodo, "but his face sure rings a bell!"

How do zombies like their roast beef served?
In gravey!

Mummy, I don't like cousin Fred.
Well leave him and eat the chips.

Why does everyone hate Dracula?
He's a pain in the neck!

What's green and warty and has two wheels?
A swamp monster on a bike!

How do elves get indigestion?
Goblin their food!

What do zombies like for pudding?
I – scream!

What sings, terrorises theatres and weighs 25 stone?
The fat-tum of the opera!

What football team do swamp monsters support?
Slitherpool!

What does Dracula have for breakfast?
Readyneck!

Quasimodo was sitting at the tea table when Mrs Quasimodo walked in carrying a Chinese wok.
"Oh, no, Esmerelda!" moaned the hunchback. "Not Chinese food again!"
"No," said his wife. "I'm just going to iron one of your shirts!"

"What do you fancy tonight – Chinese or Indian?"

What does the beast from fifty thousand fathoms like to eat?
Fish an' ships!

A vampire, a werewolf and a zombie cornered a man in a dark alleyway.
"Do you have any last requests?" asked the zombie.
"Yes," said the man. "I'd like to sing a song."
"Okay," said the zombie, "go ahead."
"Nine million, nine hundred and ninety nine thousand, nine hundred and ninety
nine green bottles, hanging on the wall . . ."

A strange blue creature from outer space walked into a corner shop.
"Hi!" said the alien. "I need to buy a few things."
"That's . . . er . . . fine," said the shopkeeper, "as long as you have the
money to pay me with."
"Oh, I've got plenty money," said the creature. "Now, I'd like four boxes of
chocolates, a dozen bottles of lemonade, fourteen blocks of chocolate ice cream,
two dozen blocks of raspberry ripple . . ."
"Excuse me," said the shopkeeper, "but are you sure you can pay for this?"
"No problem," said the creature. "Got change for a forty million zooblik note?"

What lives in the Thames and terrifies half of London?
Jack the Kipper!

What happens if you sleep with your head under the pillow?
The fairies whip all your teeth out!

What's a swamp monster's favourite drink?
Slime cordial!

What's the last thing Dracula says to his victims?
It's been nice gnawing you!

St Trinians School,
Anarchy Way,
Simpleton,
Berks.

Loadsamoney!

I used to be your Maths Teacher, boy, and look where I've ended up working now! Pay attention, you cretin! Do you think I'm writing this for the good of my health?

I should have known back when you were still just Loadsapocketmoney that you'd get yourself involved in some disreputable schemes! First you go out and earn loadsamoney (which is loads and loads more than I make!!) then you write an introduction to the Red Nose Joke Book which contains vile jokes about TEACHERS — the most wonderful beings on the face of the earth!

I always knew you were a good-for-nothing lout and, of course, I was right because TEACHERS are never wrong! Without me you wouldn't even be able to count the dosh in your wad. Mind you, you probably can't count it all anyway, you've got so much!!

The only jokes in the book that did make me laugh were the animal jokes because they reminded me of my pupils who are all nasty, vicious little animals — and you were the worst!

By the way, are you free to plaster my kitchen ceiling next Wednesday?

Yours educationally,

Miss Spelling

Miss Spelling.

TEACHER – "At Waterloo, where did Napoleon keep his armies?"
SILLY BILLY – "Up his sleevies!"

$6 + 2 + 4 + 8 = 21$ ✗ WRONG!!

TEACHER – "If I cut a banana into four pieces, an apple into six pieces and an orange into ten pieces, what will I have?"
MANDY – "A fruit salad!"

$12 \div 4 = 3$ ✓

TEACHER – "If I gave you four hamsters today and then tomorrow I gave you five, how many would you have?"
WALLY – "Eleven, miss!"
TEACHER – "Eleven?"
WALLY – "Yes, miss. I've got two already!"

TEACHER – "Wally, can you find Australia on the map?"
WALLY – "Yes, that's it down at the bottom, sir."
TEACHER – "Good. Now, Billy, who discovered Australia?"
SILLY BILLY – "Wally did, sir!"

TEACHER – "If you've got fifty pence in one pocket and seventy five pence in the other, what have you got?"

TERRY – "Someone else's trousers, miss!"

TEACHER – "Terry, if you have six bars of chocolate and your sister asks you for two, how many would you be left with?"

TERRY – "Six!"

SICK NOTE

TEACHER: You must be the new boy, where do you come from?
BOY: I'm frae Scotland, Miss.
TEACHER: What part?
BOY: All o' me, Miss.

TEACHER – "In which battle was Nelson killed?"
SILLY BILLY – "His last one, Miss!"

WHAT A MESS! SEE ME AFTER SCHOOL!

Teacher: Who wrote "To A Field Mouse?"
Pupil: Robert Burns, Miss, but I bet he didn't get an answer!

The teacher had just spent an hour explaining to his class how heat made things expand and cold made them shrink.

"Now, then," he said. "Can you give me an example of this, Elizabeth?"

"Yes, sir!" said Elizabeth. "In summer the days are long and in winter they're short!"

DAD – "Another bad report from your teacher! When I was at school, I was the teacher's pet!"
WALLY – "Oh? Couldn't she afford a real monkey, then?"

"Mother, I can't go to school today!" he sobbed. "I hate it! I can't stand it! It's awful and nobody likes me! I'm not going!"

"But you must go, dear," said his mother. "After all, you are the headmaster!"

As all the pupils trooped into her class one day the teacher was surprised to see one of them, little Mary, swathed in bandages.

"Mary!" exclaimed the teacher. "What on earth happened to you?"

"I was injured doing my homework essay, miss," Mary explained.

"What do you mean?" asked the teacher.

"You told us to write an essay on our favourite animal and I fell off the horse!"

TEACHER — "Traditionally, where have all the kings and queens of England been crowned?"

SILLY BILLY — "On their heads, miss!"

DAD — "Your history marks are rotten! When I was young history was my best subject!"

DIANA — "Ah, but when you were young there was so much less history to learn!"

TEACHER — "Now, Terry, if you had six apples and someone took three, what would you have then?"

TERRY — "A punch-up!"

SEE ME
AGAIN!!

If you've just wet yourself laughing,
you can use this page to mop it up!!

HAMLET

OMELETTE

Teacher: What do most 16th century poets have in common?
Pupil: Most of them are dead, Miss!

A boy stood up and headed for the door of the classroom while the teacher was halfway through a lesson on English Grammar.
"Where do you think you are going, boy?" asked the teacher.
"I got to go to the toilet, sir," the boy replied.
"No, no, no!" scolded the teacher. "That's wrong! I HAVE to go to the toilet. You HAVE to go to the toilet. She HAS to go to the toilet. He HAS to go to the toilet. We all HAVE to go to the toilet."
"Blimey, sir. Think there'll be enough paper?"

2/10 MUST DO BETTER !

TEACHER – "You're an hour late, boy! Where have you been?"
WALLY – "Sorry, sir. A sign on the escalator said 'Dogs must be carried' and it took me ages to find one!"

A cross-eyed teacher was called to the headmaster's office one morning. Immediately the teacher arrived.

"Come in, Miss Jones," said the headmaster as the teacher arrived. Immediately his gaze was drawn to her alarming cross-eyed stare.

"I'm afraid," said the headmaster, "that I'll have to ask you to give up teaching, Miss Jones."

"But why?" said the cross-eyed teacher, looking straight at the headmaster and right out the window. "I have excellent qualifications, I studied hard at university, I work extra hours after school . . ."

"Yes, I know all that," said the headmaster, "but you still can't control your pupils!"

TEACHER – "What do you find on the outside of a tree?"
WALLY – "Don't know, sir."
TEACHER – "Bark, boy! Bark!"
WALLY – "Woof! Woof!"

$8 \times 12 = 47$ **✗** WRONG

TEACHER – "When was Henry the Eighth born?"
SILLY BILLY – "Um . . . on his birthday, miss!?"

TEACHER – "Where would you see the English Channel?"
WALLY – "Don't know, miss."
TEACHER – "You don't know?"
WALLY – "No, miss. We only get the four usual channels on our telly!"

TEACHER: Susan, I told you to draw a horse and carriage and you've only drawn the horse.
SUSAN: I know, Miss – the horse will draw the carriage!

MUM –"Why are you so late home, Carol?"
CAROL – "I was kept behind in school because I didn't know where the Pyrenees were."
MUM – "Well, where did you leave them?"

TEACHER – "Who defeated the Philistines?"
WALLY – "No idea, sir. I don't watch American football."

Teacher: What family does the Orang Utan belong to?
Pupil: Well no one down our street's got one, Miss!

TEACHER — "And what did Christopher Columbus say before setting off to discover America?
SILLY BILLY — "Um . . . all aboard?"

TEACHER — "Billy, I think you've got your wellies on the wrong feet."
SILLY BILLY — "But these are the only feet I've got, miss!"

TEACHER – "Give me the names of ten animals you would find on a farm."
WALLY – "A cow, a chicken, a pig, a goat and . . . er . . . six sheep!"

Dunknocking,
22 Ringading Road,
Dongcaster.

Dear Sir,

Knock-knock? Knock-knock? What is it with all this Knock-knock stuff? Are you trying to drive me out of business? As the biggest manufacturer of bells in the country, I employ 52½ people (Gladys the tea lady is only part time). Where would they be without bells? Going Knock-knock! on the door of the dole office, that's where!

You can't go around encouraging people to knock instead of ring with all your silly Knock-knock gags. What would happen if cyclists yelled **"Knock-knock"** instead of ringing a bell when a pedestrian got in the way? The poor pedestrian would just have time to turn round and say "Who's there?" then WHAM! He wakes up in hospital with bits of bicycle wedged in his bottom!

And what about the traditional British Sunday? It wouldn't be the same if you drove us bell makers out of business. The sound of church bells on a crisp winter's morning could not be replaced by the vicar climbing the church spire and screaing **"KNOCK-KNOCK!"** at the top of his voice, could it?

The thing that upsets me most is that there's no need for these jokes to start off with Knock-knock at all. They could just as easily start off Ding-Dong, like this:

> Ding-Dong!
> Who's there?
> Alison.
> Alison who?
> Alison to bells all the time!

See? For goodness sake cut all this Knock-knock rubbish and get in some decent bell jokes. Your horror section, for example, has some fine jokes featuring Quasimodo, the well-known campinologist.

More bell jokes – you have been tolled! (Get it?)

Yours ringingly,

Benjamin Tinkles

Benjamin Tinkles
(Big Ben to my friends)

KNOCK! KNOCK!

Knock! Knock!
Who's there?
Fire!
Fire who? And what's that burning smell?

Knock! Knock!
Who's there?
Alf.
Alf who?
Alf time at the football match!

Knock! Knock!
Who's there?
Alex.
Alex who?
Alex plain later!

Knock! Knock!
Who's there?
Th-th-th-th ...
Th-th-th-th who?
Th-th-th-th-th-th ...

Knock! Knock!
Who's there?
Kent.
Kent who?
Kent you tell?

Knock! Knock!
Who's there?
Boo.
Boo who?
There, there, no need to cry!

Knock! Knock!
Who's there?
Alf.
Not Alf time at the football match again?
No, it's the second Alf!

Knock! Knock!
Who's there?
Ben.
Ben who?
Ben waitin' here for ages!

Knock! Knock!
Who's there?
Hugh.
Hugh who?
Hugh rent's due so open up

Knock! Knock!
Who's there?
Handsome.
Handsome who?
Handsome money over! It's the rent man again!

Knock! Knock!
Who's there?
Amanda.
Amanda who?
Amanda fix da bell!

Knock! Knock!
Who's there?
Th-th-th-th …
Th-th-th-th who?
Th-th-th-th-th-th …

← OBSERVANT
READERS WILL
HAVE NOTICED
THAT THIS JOKE
IS IN THE
WRONG
SECTION.

Knock! Knock!
Who's there?
Ernie.
Ernie who?
Ernie body in?

What goes **RING-WO**B B L E! **RING-WO**B B L E!
A jellyphone.

Knock! Knock!
Who's there?
Otto.
Otto who?
Otto know, but I forgot!

THE WORLD'S LARGEST
KNOCK! KNOCK! JOKE ;..

Knock! Knock!
Who's there?
Luke.
Luke who?
Luke an' see, you wally!

Knock! Knock!
Who's there?
Hugh.
Hugh who?
Coo-eee!!

Knock! Knock!
Who's there?
Wanda.
Wanda who?
Wanda open up yet?

Knock! Knock!
Who's there?
Isabel.
Isabel who?
Isabel not working yet?

THE SMALLEST... →

Knock! Knock!
Who's there?
Anya.
Anya who?
Anya ever goin' to let me in?

Knock! Knock!
Who's there?
Lady.
Lady who?
I didn't know you could yodel!

Knock! Knock!
Who's there?
Stan.
Stan who?
Stan back, I'm gonna smash the door down!

THE WORST ↰

Knock! Knock!
Who's there?
A twit.
A twit who?
You got an owl in there?

Knock! Knock!
Who's there?
Igor.
Igor who?
I gorra shock off your bell!

Knock! Knock!
Who's there?
Th-th-th-th ...
Th-th-th-th who?
Th-th-th-th-th-th ...

Knock! Knock!
Who's there?
Police!
Police who?
Police let me in, it's cold out here!

Knock! Knock!
Who's there?
Amos.
Amos who?
A mosquito!

Knock! Knock!
Who's there?
Signor.
Signor who?
Signor light on, so I thought I'd drop by!

Knock! Knock!
Who's there?
Th-th-ma …
Th-the-ma who?
Th-m-man w-with the st-stu-st … Aw, forget it!!

Smash! Smash!
Who's there?
Hook Hand Harry!

Knock! Knock!
Who's there?
Jim.
Jim who?
Jimmake everyone stand about out here?

THE LAST ONE

Knock! Knock!
Get knotted!

Dear Subject,

Buckingham Palace,
London.

We were most concerned when we learned that you were to be including a section of jokes about animals in your rather splendid book.

As spokesperson for the Palace Dogs, we feel we must say that we are not amused!

You must not make fun of poor animals in this manner. Animals suffer enough at the hands of humans without you poking fun at them. Have you ever had an enormous Scots Guardsman crunch your tail with a marching boot whilst you were officially welcoming the King of Sweden? We have, and we can assure you that if we had interrupted the ceremony with even the tiniest whimper, we'd have been off to the Royal Vet before our paws could touch the ground.

You will notice that we have had the Royal we quite a lot on this page. We apologise for this — we usually only have the Royal we on the Royal lamp post.

Despite the animal jokes and despite the fact that we prefer cold wet noses to big red ones, we found the nonsense jokes absolutely spiffing, especially the one about putting the cat out!

Yours rulingly,

Corgi R.

What's pink and black, has four wings, four feet and won't let you come near?
A pair of sunburnt penguins!

The owner of a small cafe was surprised to see a very well dressed gorilla walk in one day.
"I'd like a banana sandwich, please," said the gorilla.
"Er . . . yes, sir," said the cafe owner. "That will be £3.50, please, and may I say that it's a pleasure to serve you. We . . . er . . . don't get many gorillas in here."
"Well," grunted the gorilla, "at £3.50 for a banana sandwich I'm not surprised!"

MOTHER – "Sharon! I thought I told you to change the water in the goldfish bowl?"
SHARON – "But, Mum, they haven't drunk the last lot yet!"

What do you get if you cross a budgie with a shark?
A flying fish that says "Who's a pretty boy, then?" and bites your arm off!

What's the difference between a buffalo and a bison?
You can't wash your hands in a buffalo!

What do you call a loony blackbird?
Raven mad!

Why do birds fly south for the winter?
'Cos it's too far to walk!

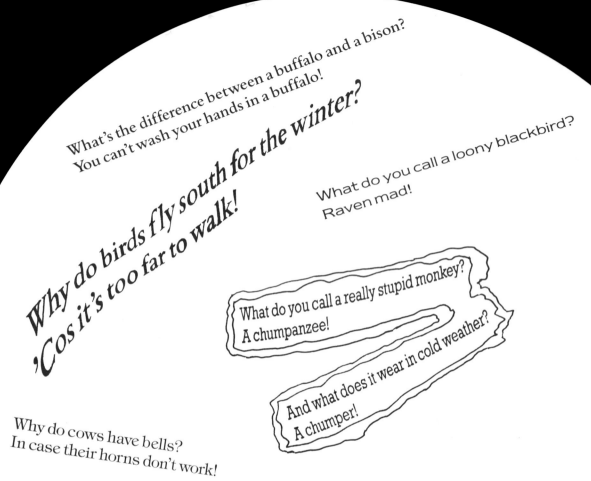

What do you call a really stupid monkey?
A chumpanzee!

And what does it wear in cold weather?
A chumper!

Why do cows have bells?
In case their horns don't work!

The captain of the ocean liner Titanic was watching a magician rehearsing his
act for the cabaret that evening. The magician produced a dove from a hat
and placed it on a perch. The captain applauded the impressive trick, but the
sudden noise frightened the dove which flew out of an open porthole, never to
be seen again.

What's got four legs, a mane, a tail and wears roller skates?
A horse (I lied about the roller skates).

"What am I going to do?" moaned the magician. "That was the only bird I had!"
"No problem," said the captain. "Our engineer has a parrot. You can borrow that."
That evening the magician started his cabaret show in front of the assembled
passengers. To great applause, he produced the parrot from the hat and placed
it on the perch. Continuing his act, he made an egg disappear. The audience was
impressed, but the parrot wasn't.

Why do hippos wear nighties?
Their pyjamas are in the washing!

What do you call a man who puts his right arm into a lion's mouth?
Lefty!

"It's up his sleeve! It's up his sleeve!" squawked the parrot.
"Shut up!" hissed the magician. He then made a bunch of flowers disappear.
"It's in his coat! It's in his coat!" squawked the parrot.

What's the difference between an elephant and a biscuit?
You can't dip an elephant in your tea!

What's the best way to catch a rabbit?
Hide behind a wall and make a noise like a lettuce!

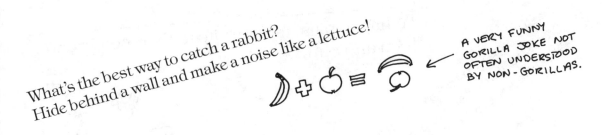

A VERY FUNNY
GORILLA JOKE NOT
OFTEN UNDERSTOOD
BY NON-GORILLAS.

What's the difference between an elephant and a plate of peas?
An elephant won't roll off the end of your fork!

What do aardvark's have that nothing else has?
Baby aardvarks!

Just then, the ship hit an iceberg and sank. The magician ended up on a liferaft
alone, and the parrot fluttered down to perch beside him. For a while there was
silence, then the parrot turned to the magician.
"Okay, smarty pants," he said, "what did you do with the ship?"

What has fifty legs but can't walk?
Half a centipede!

What do pigs use to write to their pen friends?
Pen and oink!

PIG PEN →

"Aah!" screamed Father running in from the garden. "I've just been stung by a wasp!"
"You should put some cream on it," said Mother.
"Don't be stupid!" said Father. "It'll be miles away by now!"

A chicken sat outside the hen house watching the farmer arriving home from the weekly market. The farmer looked very pleased and was clutching a handful of money. As he crossed the farmyard, he shouted to his wife, "Guess what? Eggs are going up again!"
And the chicken fainted . . .

What dance do ducks like?
The quackstep!

Which side of a zebra has the most stripes?
The outside!

What goes PECK-PECK-PECK-PECK-BANG!
A chicken in a minefield.

But, Mum! All the other kids take friends home to play!

What's grey and has a trunk?
A mouse going on holiday!

What do you get if you cross a Highland cow with an army general?
A military coo!

Two little birds were sitting in their nest when a jet aeroplane roared past at top speed.
"Crucial!" whistled the first bird. "He was really movin'!"
"Yeah," agreed the second. "You would too if your bum was on fire!"

What's brown and has a trunk?
The mouse coming home again!

Why wouldn't Noah let the two maggots in the apple on board the ark?
'Cos he only took animals in pairs!

What's grey with a pink ribbon?
A gift-wrapped shark!

What's pink, lives in the sea and carries a machine gun?
Al Caprawn.

What do you get if you cross a gorilla with the white of an egg?
A Meringue Utan!

A duck waddled into Boots one day and gave a loud quack to attract the assistant's attention.

"Excuse me, miss," he said. "Do you have anything for sore beaks?"

"Er, well . . ." said the assistant. "You could try this lip cream. That should do the job."

"Fine," said the duck. "I'll take it. Would you put it on my bill?"

HA! HA! THIS ONE'S A QUACKER!!

Why do giraffes have such long necks?
To join their heads to their bodies, you wally!

Why do storks lift one leg?
'Cos if they lifted both legs, they'd fall over!

How can you tell a worm's head from its tail?
Tickle it and see which end giggles!

How do you stop a rhinoceros from charging things?
Hide his American Express card!

"What do you mean you want to complain? There's nothing wrong with the dog. When I sold him to you I told you he'd probably grow another two feet!"

THE SERIOUS BIT!
A message from Comic Relief

Last year the Comic Relief appeal raised over £15 million. We promised that all the money raised would go directly to help communities in Africa and young people in crisis in the UK – AND IT DID …

In Africa
We promised that money would go to help find clean water for people to drink in Wollo, the dry region in Ethiopia. IT HAS, through the Oxfam programme. The villagers build the wells, Comic Relief pays for the pumps and the technicians.

We promised that money would go to help immunise children against diseases like tuberculosis, typhoid, polio and measles. IT HAS – Save The Children, funded by Comic Relief, helps with programmes in Ethiopia, Sudan and Somalia.

We promised that money would go to save villages threatened by soil erosion. IT HAS – Oxfam projects in Somalia have been funded by Comic Relief to help village communities solve their own problems.

In the UK
We promised that money would go to help young people who are homeless. By helping projects like Shelter in Scotland, which helps young people to provide their own homes, and other projects that provide hostels where people can stay while they look for work, IT HAS.

We promised that money would go to help the disabled. By helping to fund schemes for teaching disabled people to drive in Northern Ireland and by providing meeting places for the handicapped up and down the country, IT HAS.

We promised that money would go to help the thousands of young people addicted to alcohol, drugs and solvents. By helping Charity Projects fund detoxification centres and the provision of longer term help and support, IT HAS.

This Year
We are continuing our work in Africa and the UK, stretching our interests to cover the whole of Africa and expanding our work in the UK to take in elderly people as well as the young.

Remember!
All of the money sent to Comic Relief will go straight to help people in Africa and the UK. None of it goes on salaries or administration expenses because all of that is sponsored.